Life Is a Gift

HOW TO USE

AFFIRMATIONS TO TRANSFORM
YOUR LIFE

ALIYAH KAMALA

Copyright © 2016 by Aliyah Kamala

Kamala & Company LLC
Atlanta, GA

All rights reserved including the right of reproduction in whole or in part in any form.

ISBN-13: 978-0692717219

I dedicate this book to my children
Jakwai, Shakayah, & Amir.

Acknowledgements

Give thanks to the Most High for the guidance, grace, & insight to complete & publish this project. Thank you to all of my dear family, friends, & community who are a part of my village, constantly providing love, support, & inspiration.

Salutation to the Dawn

Look to this day,

For it is life,

The very life of life.

Within its brief span lies all the verities & realities,

Of your existence.

The bliss of growth,

The glory of action,

The splendor of beauty.

For yesterday is but a dream,

And tomorrow is but a vision .

Yet today well lived,

Makes every yesterday a dream of happiness,

And every tomorrow a vision of hope,

Look well therefore to this day.

-Attributed to Kalidasa
Translated from Sanskrit

Introduction

An affirmation is a declaration that something exists or is true. It is a positive self-talk statement that expresses a desired outcome.

Affirmations are a form of inspiration, encouragement, and motivation. For example, if your goal is to travel the world, a possible way to affirm that desire would be to say "I am a world traveler who enjoys exploring exciting new places." With consistent use, affirmations can be a great way to create powerful transformation in your life. By helping to eliminate negative thoughts & behaviors, affirmations represent a major key on the path of personal growth & development.

When you use affirmations every day it's like being your own personal cheerleader, where you can access inspiration at any time through positive thinking. Affirmations offer an opportunity to enhance your inner dialogue by aligning your words with the highest vision that you have for your life. It is said that what you focus on expands. In this way, positive affirmations can help you to manifest your desires through intention and the Law of Attraction. The Law of Attraction basically states that "like attracts like." In other words, in order to create what you desire, you must first become what you desire through your thoughts, words, & actions. The key is to use the power of intention, positive words, & inspired action consistently. As a result, you will be able to manifest wellness, abundance, & success in every aspect of your life.

Affirmations are a way to use goal-oriented statements to help reprogram your subconscious mind in order to manifest your desires. They are an anecdote for negative thinking. Your positive words are deliberately shaping your positive world. As we focus on connecting the intentions of the heart and mind, the words we choose to utter are a direct reflection of the life we live. Connect to what brings joy to your life & use words of enthusiasm and encouragement to help activate your affirmations. Embody the words you speak and watch your experiences unfold as a reflection of your most dominant thoughts.

How to Use this Book

You can go through this book in sequential order or choose affirmations at random based on what resonates with you the best. Feel free to work with one affirmation for the day or more than one. It is a personal choice that is based on your current needs. Recite your affirmations at least 3 times every morning and every night before bedtime in order to achieve maximum results. Every morning & evening say, visualize, & feel the affirmations that connect with you the most. Move through your day & keep your positive declarations with you by simply thinking about them or having visual reminders in your surroundings.

Having visual cues of your affirmations around such as index cards, sticky notes, or pictures, help you to be deliberate in the unfolding of your goals. Consistency is key when it comes to getting results from using positive

self-talk. Also, the "secret sauce" to success with affirming your desires is to imagine what it would feel like if what you were declaring was

happening at this very moment. Act as if your goals are already achieved. Incorporate all of your senses when saying your affirmations. Say your positive statements with deep conviction and enthusiasm. Leave no space for doubt, worry, or fear. Whenever a negative thought or emotion arises, allow yourself to feel it, release it, & then move on to a better feeling thought. The key is to shift your focus from problem to solution by activating your positive

affirmations. Allow yourself to experience all of the emotions and feelings associated with what you would like to manifest and that will help to draw those desires to you faster.

Benefits of
Positive Affirmations

-Create a positive mood & state of mind.

-Help to build confidence.

-Stimulate your creative subconscious which will start generating creative ideas to help you achieve your goals.

-Program your brain to more readily perceive and recognize what is required to go after your dreams.

-Activate the Law of Attraction, thereby drawing into your life the people, resources, and circumstances for you to accomplish your goals.

-Builds your internal motivation to take the necessary actions to achieve your desires.

-Helps to overcome negative thinking & counterproductive behavior patterns.

In addition to saying your affirmations daily, you may also choose to:

-Post affirmations around your house, car, or workspace as a reminder to move through the day with intention.

-Turn your affirmations into a screensaver on any of the electronic devices that you use.

-Record your affirmations and listen to them at any time throughout the day.

-Create an "Affirmations Book" by writing out each of your affirmations in a notebook. Include drawings, pictures, and visuals to help bring them to life.

-Create a poster board collage of your positive affirmations.

6 Daily Practices to Enhance Your Affirmations

-Meditation

-Visualization

-Gratitude & appreciation

-Journaling

-Creating a sacred space for quiet reflection

-Surrounding yourself with positive people

~ 1 ~

I experience miracles each & every day.

~2~

My life is a perfect balance of effort & ease.

~3~

I am fully embracing what empowers me.

I am easily releasing what does not serve my highest good.

~4~

Every day I show up

as the best

version of myself.

~5~

I am living

the life of my dreams

& loving every

moment of it.

~6~

I am clear & confident

in asking for

what I want.

I deserve the best

of all things.

~7~

Moving through the day
with a deep sense
of gratitude
& appreciation
keeps me in the
flow of abundance.

~8~

It feels good

to be

surrounded by

positive people.

~9~

I am taking

bold steps

in the direction

of my goals.

~10~

I practice patience in every part of my life.

~ 11 ~

I am expanding

my awareness

through daily

meditation.

~12~

Gratitude is my daily practice. Abundance is my way of life.

~13~

I am surrounded

by the healing

power of love.

My heart is overflowing

with joy & gratitude.

~14~

It feels good

to move through

the day with

passion & purpose.

~15~

Deep breathing is the soundtrack to my day.

~16~

Inspiration is all around me. I am using my creative energy to design the life of my dreams.

~17~

I release
the need to
overextend myself.
I do what I can
to empower &
inspire others.

~18~

I practice forgiveness in every part of my life.

~19~

I am in

the right place,

at the right time,

giving & receiving

in the flow

of abundance.

~20~

I attentively listen to my inner voice. I trust my gut feeling & honor my intuition.

~21~

My relationships
are filled with
love & harmony.
I am empowered
and supported by my
circle of influence.

… # ~22~

I am ready

& prepared

for massive success.

~23~

It feels good to move through the day with a positive mental attitude.

~24~

I am open to receive all the positive support that comes my way.

~25~

I welcome

new opportunities

to learn, grow,

& prosper.

~26~

Each day I choose to be sincere & genuine in every aspect of my life. I am committed to showing up & doing my best.

~27~

I am a good listener. There is value in offering my undivided attention.

~28~

I am clearing

my space &

making room for

the next best thing.

~29~

I love taking good care of myself. Every day I drink at least 8 glasses of water. It feels great to be healthy & hydrated.

~30~

I spend time in nature every day. I feel energized & refreshed enjoying the sunshine & breathing fresh air. I am surrounded by the beauty of nature.

~31~

It feels amazing to exercise every day. I am committed to maintaining a healthy lifestyle.

~32~

I am creatively using the resources around me to maximize my success.

~33~

Every day I challenge myself to move outside of my comfort zone.

~34~

I am committed to consistently saving & investing at least 10% of my income every month. It feels great to build wealth.

~35~

I have unlimited earning potential. I easily capitalize on my creative ideas.

~36~

I am using the power of meditation, deep breathing, & yoga to radically enhance my wellness.

~37~

With effort & ease

I happily create what

I truly desire .

~38~

I am learning & growing in every part of my life.

~39~

Every day I take time

to relax, release,

& recharge.

~40~

It feels great to spend quality time with my friends & family.

~ 41 ~

I am willing to do what it takes to get the job done. I am committed to excellence in everything that I do.

~42~

I visualize what I want

& act on it with

passion & enthusiasm.

~43~

I am planting seeds

of good fortune

in thought,

word, & deed.

~44~

Today I am making

an effort to

arrive early to where

ever I need to be.

~45~

I am willing to
face the truth
even when it's difficult.
Through awareness
I am empowered
to make changes.

~46~

I choose to think big.

I choose to take risks.

I choose to speak with the utmost conviction & to hold my vision until it comes to pass.

~47~

I am grateful that my life is overflowing with abundance.

I give from a place of plenty.

~48~

Every day I give thanks for all that I have in my life.

~49~

It feels good to support those who support me.

~50~

I am easily & effortlessly attracting money into my life. I am building a strong legacy of wealth through my daily financial habits.

~51~

My life is filled with love & bliss.

I am centered.

I am grounded.

~52~

Every day I take time to celebrate my wins.

~53~

I am embracing

the ebb & flow

of life.

~54~

It feels good

to be in the

best shape

of my life.

~55~

I feel confident & empowered. I am transforming all excuses into inspired action.

~56~

I am attracting loving experiences into my life.

~57~-

I am fully
supported in all things.
I have all that
I need to make
a positive impact &
accomplish my goals.

~58~

Self-care

is my

daily practice.

~59~

I am using the

power of prayer

in every

part of my life.

~60~

It feels good
to move through
the day
with gratitude
& appreciation.

~ 61 ~

I have more

than enough time,

energy, & resources

to do what I love.

~62~

Every day I take time to nourish my mind, body, & soul.

~63~

I am open &

receptive to new

perspectives & ideas

that inspire me

to think big.

~64~

I easily release stress from my mind, body, & soul.

~65~

I am shifting

my focus from

doing to being.

~66~

The constant abundance I experience is an outward expression of my inner wealth.

~67~

I use my smile to

radiate joy

everywhere

that I go.

~68~

Each day I listen to music that is inspiring & uplifting.

~69~

With faith, confidence, & determination, I am positioning myself to win.

~70~

I have the power to transform my life through thought, word, & deed.

~71~

I am

enthusiastic

about life.

~72~

It feels good

to move

through the day

with vibrant energy.

~73~

I AM enough.

I DO enough.

I HAVE enough.

~74~

It feels good to successfully complete what I start.

~75~

My life is a beautiful adventure filled with fun & excitement.

~76~

I am enjoying the journey.

~77~

Each day I harness the healing power of laughter.

~78~

My life is an expression of love & grace.

~79~

I am patient with the flow of life. I am at ease knowing that everything happens in divine order.

~80~

I deserve the best of all things. I demand & require the highest respect.

~ 81 ~

I attract prosperous

people into my life.

I am surrounded

by wealth & abundance.

~82~

I am nurturing

my dreams daily

with clear vision,

positive affirmations,

& inspired action.

~83~

I am

going with the flow

& trusting the process.

~84~

I fully embrace tranquility as a way of life.

~85~

I am grateful

for the abundance

of love that

surrounds me.

~86~

It feels great

to be a thoughtful

& caring friend.

~87~

I am embracing healthy ways to channel negative feelings & emotions.

~88~

I enjoy my own company. It's okay for me to be alone at times.

~89~

It feels good

to take time to

get to know myself.

I honor my interests

& preferences.

~90~

I am enthusiastically visualizing my goals & acting as if they are already achieved.

~ 91 ~

I look at all challenges as opportunities to make improvements.

~92~

I release the need

to compare

myself to others.

~93~

Despite any fear that is present, I am courageously moving in the direction of my goals with focus & inspired action.

~94~

I am watching my visions & goals unfold right before my eyes with gratitude & appreciation.

~95~

I avoid procrastination & use my time to prepare, organize, & take action.

~96~

I feel empowered

in claiming

victory over my

circumstances.

~97~

I am safe

where ever I travel.

~98~

It feels good to eat the best quality organic whole foods that nature has to offer.

~99~

My thoughts, words, & actions are in alignment with what I want to experience.

~100~

Every day I am making healthy choices to support my wellness.

~101~

I easily remain calm in the midst of challenging situations.

~102~

I am sharing

my gifts

& honoring

my legacy

through service.

~103~

I acknowledge where there is need for improvement & make a commitment to do better.

~104~

Good vibes

are the soundtrack

to my day.

~105~

I treat each moment as a precious gift.

~106~

I am nurturing

my relationships

by showing up

& honoring my

agreements.

~107~

My life is

free of lack

& limitation.

I openly give

& receive.

~108~

It feels great to be healthy, wealthy, & successful.

~109~

My home is a place of peace. My home is filled with warmth, comfort, & love.

~110~

I am embracing

my dreams &

expanding the vision

that I have for my life.

~111~

Every day I take time

to write down &

review my goals.

~112~

I am asking the right questions & getting the answers I need to grow & prosper.

~113~

I easily find joy & comfort within myself. I know that love is an inside job.

~114~

I am my own best friend.

~115~

It feels good

to travel, explore, &

learn new things.

~116~

I am worthy of success.

~117~

All my needs are being met in a major way.

~118~

I know that

life is a gift.

I rejoice in all

that I have.

~119~

I use joy as my guiding light to harness the power of happiness.

~120~

I support myself in loving ways.

~121~

Compassion & forgiveness reside in my heart. My life is an expression of unconditional love.

~122~

I choose to make the best of what I am presented with today.

~123~

My heart & mind are aligned in perfect harmony.

~124~

It feels good
to be healthy,
whole, & vibrant.
I am taking
great care of myself.

~125~

My thoughts, words, & actions are in alignment with the highest vision that I have for my life.

~126~

Love begins with me. The more I love myself, the more love I have to give to others.

~127~

I am creating

my best life

in thought, word,

& deed.

~128~

I am open & receptive to see the lesson in all things. I am learning as I grow.

~129~

My consistent daily habits are creating positive changes in my life.

~130~

I am clear about what I truly desire. I state my wants & needs with confidence.

~131~

It feels amazing to define myself by my own standard of beauty.

~132~

I lovingly embrace

what brings joy

to my life.

~133~

I am

getting better

with each day.

~134~

It feels good to

be calm, clear,

& grounded.

~135~

I am open to new beginnings.
I am embracing change & adventure.

~136~

My positive thoughts are shaping my positive world.

~137~

I am happily releasing the stress of other people's problems.

~138~

I am making wellness my top priority & watching everything else fall into place.

~139~

I am fully

supported

by loving

relationships.

~140~

I expect good things to happen in my life.

~141~

My mind is conditioned

for success.

I surrender to

the process &

create with ease.

~142~

I am headed in the right direction & making progress every day.

~143~

I release the past & embrace this moment of the present. I am excited about what life has to offer.

~144~

I am building strength & confidence daily by taking full responsibility for my life.

~145~

I say what's on my heart & speak with sincerity.

~146~

I am focused, disciplined, & consistent. It feels great to be at the top of my game.

~147~

I experience joy

in every part

of my life.

~148~

I am learning to

love myself more &

more each day.

~149~

It feels good

to smile & laugh.

My life is exciting.

~150~

I AM amazing.

I FEEL amazing.

I LOOK amazing.

Tips for Creating Your Own Positive Affirmations

-Write them in the present tense.

Example: I am driving the car of my dreams.

Opposed to: I will be driving the car of my dreams.

Make your affirmations come to life by acting as if they are happening in the now.

-Avoid using words of negation like

   no, not, un, & don't.

Example: I am supporting my wellness by maintaining a healthy weight. Opposed to: I don't want to be overweight.

-Make them short and to the point.

1 to 3 brief sentences will get the job done.

-Focus on what you desire and want to create.

Make a list of all your dreams & goals. Transform them into positive affirming statements.

-Use feeling words charged with

   passion & enthusiasm to activate your

   emotions.

Example: wonderful, easily, gracefully, amazing, great, good, effortlessly, lovingly, joyfully, inspiring, action, transforming, growing, learning, expanding.

Create Your Own Affirmations

_____

_____

_____

_____

_____

_____

_____

_____

_____

_____

_____

_____

_____

_____

Create Your Own Affirmations

_____

_____

_____

_____

_____

_____

_____

_____

_____

_____

_____

_____

_____

_____

Create Your Own Affirmations

_____

_____

_____

_____

_____

_____

_____

_____

_____

_____

_____

_____

_____

Create Your Own Affirmations

_____

_____

_____

_____

_____

_____

_____

_____

_____

_____

_____

_____

_____

_____

Contact:

Websites

www.lifeisagiftbook.com

www.aliyahkamala.com

Social Media

@AliyahKamala

Email

aliyahkamala@gmail.com

Business Phone:

678-421-4106

To: Sanaa

May this book be a source of inspiration for you.

Aly ♥
2/1/24

Made in the USA
Columbia, SC
07 May 2021